BUNYIP VS. CHUPACABRA

by Golriz Golkar

CAPSTONE PRESS
a capstone imprint

Published by Capstone Press, an imprint of Capstone
1710 Roe Crest Drive, North Mankato, Minnesota 56003
capstonepub.com

Copyright © 2026 by Capstone. All rights reserved. No part of this publication may be reproduced in whole or in part, or stored in a retrieval system, or transmitted in any form or by any means, electronic, mechanical, photocopying, recording, or otherwise, without written permission of the publisher.

Library of Congress Cataloging-in-Publication Data is available on the Library of Congress website.

ISBN: 9798875225529 (hardcover)
ISBN: 9798875225475 (paperback)
ISBN: 9798875225482 (ebook PDF)

Summary: A doglike monster faces off against a creature with a long neck. These cryptids may be an equal match, but who will come out on top?

Editorial Credits
Editor: Ashley Kuehl; Designer: Hilary Wacholz; Media Researcher: Rebekah Hubstenberger; Production Specialist: Tori Abraham

Image Credits
Alamy: Andrey Panchenko, 5 (bottom), 26, 29 (chupacabra), ART Collection, 18–19, Brian Overcast, 10–11, Gibson Green, 27, Matthew Corrigan, 13, Science History Images, 5 (top); Getty Images: Big_Ryan, 25, iStock/barmah john, 20–21; Shutterstock: Alexlky, cover (bottom), cammep, 29 (crown), Daniel Eskridge, cover (top), 15, 16–17, delcarmat, 7, Happy monkey, 22–23, neftali, 9, Viktoriia_P, 6; Topfoto: Fortean, 20 (bottom left)

Design Elements
Getty Images: AdrianHillman; Shutterstock: Ballerion

Any additional websites and resources referenced in this book are not maintained, authorized, or sponsored by Capstone. All product and company names are trademarks™ or registered® trademarks of their respective holders.

Printed and bound in China. 006276

TABLE OF CONTENTS

FACE-OFF 4

SOME HISTORY 8

ALIKE AND DIFFERENT. 14

WATCH OUT! 18

SWAMPY STRUGGLE 26

> Glossary 30
>
> Read More 31
>
> Internet Sites 31
>
> Index .32
>
> About the Author 32

Words in **bold** are in the glossary.

FACE-OFF

A strange creature splashes around in a swamp. It has a long neck. Its head looks like a horse's. It crawls out of the water slowly and roars.

Suddenly, a doglike creature comes out of the trees. It flashes its large **fangs**. The monster drools from hunger. Sharp claws extend from its paws. Its eyes glow red.

It's one **cryptid** against another. Who will win—Bunyip or Chupacabra?

Name: Bunyip

Aliases: Kianpraty, Yaa-loo

Type of Cryptid: Horselike, fishlike

First Sighting: Ancient **folklore** from about 45,000 years ago

Range (Area): Australia

Likes: Tasty humans, maybe plants

Dislikes: Daylight

Name: Chupacabra
Alias: None
Type of Cryptid: Doglike, reptile
First Sighting: 1990s
Range (Area): Puerto Rico, Mexico, United States
Likes: Sucking animal blood
Dislikes: Running into humans

SOME HISTORY

The Bunyip lives in swamps and lagoons in Australia. It was first mentioned in **Aboriginal** folklore, tens of thousands of years ago. The creature ate humans who got close.

By the 1800s, people called it a Bunyip. That means "devil" or "spirit." In 1818, an English explorer discovered strange bones near a lake. They seemed to belong to an **aquatic** creature. Soon, many people were seeing the Bunyip.

The Taíno people lived in the Caribbean from around 1100 CE. They told stories of spirits that could harm people. The Taíno left stories in their cave art in Puerto Rico. Some of the art told about **vampires**. These creatures drink blood.

FACT
The Chupacabra has been spotted in Mexico, Puerto Rico, and the southwestern United States.

The first known Chupacabra sighting happened in 1995. Puerto Rican farmers found their goats and chickens dead. The animals' blood was gone.

Local people had seen a small, red-eyed creature with spikes on its back. They blamed it for the animals' deaths. They named it Chupacabra. That means "goatsucker" in Spanish.

ALIKE AND DIFFERENT

BUNYIP

Many people say the Bunyip is the size of a dog or bigger. Dark hair or fur covers its body. It has a horselike head. Its neck is long. Its body looks like a hippo or an ox. Four short legs help it swim and even walk on land. It makes a loud boom or screech.

CHUPACABRA

The Chupacabra is as big as a medium dog. It walks on four legs . . . or maybe two legs. It has a big, round head. It has big, red eyes but no eyelids. Some say it is furry. Others say it is hairless or has scaly skin. One thing is for sure: It has sharp fangs and claws!

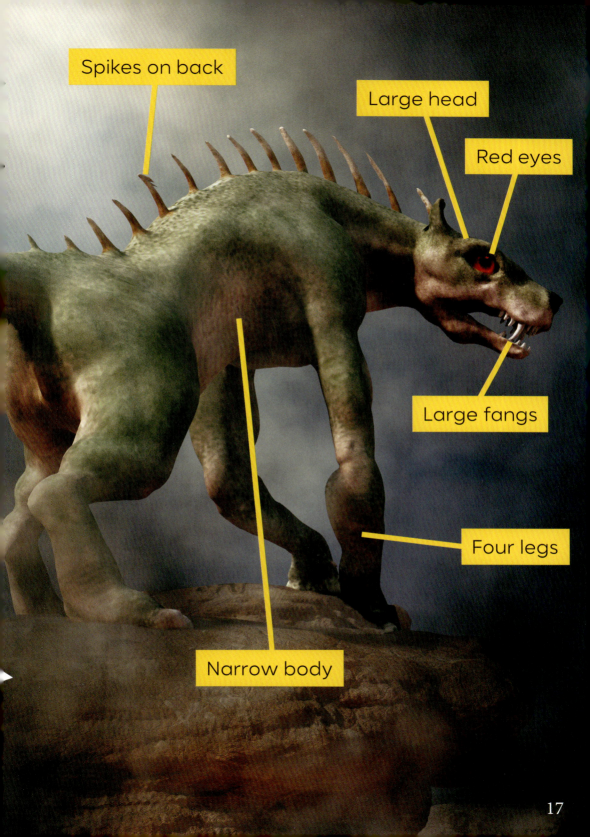

WATCH OUT!

The Bunyip is a fast swimmer. It looks for **prey** at night. It is said to like women and children best. Some say it rises from the water. It roars before an attack. Others have seen the Bunyip walk on land. They say it is shy and eats plants.

In 1845, an Aboriginal man found the body of a Bunyip. He said it had eaten his mother at a nearby lake. The man drew a picture of the cryptid he had seen. Another man recognized it. This man pointed to big cuts on his chest. He said the Bunyip had attacked him.

The Chupacabra is also fierce. Many dead sheep were found in a Puerto Rican town in 1995. They had strange cut marks and no blood.

A few months later, more than 150 farm animals were found dead in another town. Those animals had also lost their blood.

Some people said they saw the cryptid. One man said it had bitten his dog. Another person said it had ripped open a window of his house. Then it took off. Was this the creature that had hunted the animals? No one knew for sure.

SWAMPY STRUGGLE

Back to this swampy battle. The Bunyip lets out another loud roar. The Chupacabra flashes its claws, ready to pounce. Which cryptid will win the fight?

Both are strong. Their attacks are usually deadly.

The Bunyip can grab prey in water or on land. It can gobble up big prey such as humans.

The Chupacabra goes after big prey too. But it can use its fangs and claws to claim victims of any size.

The Bunyip leaps out of the water. It grabs the Chupacabra in its mouth. But the Chupacabra fights back. It claws at the Bunyip. It takes a big bite with its sharp fangs.

The Bunyip lets out a roar and plops back into the water. It disappears under the surface.

IT'S OVER! THE CHUPACABRA WINS!

BUT DO YOU AGREE? Who do you think would win when

the Bunyip and Chupacabra CLASH?

GLOSSARY

Aboriginal (ab-uh-RIJ-uh-nuhl)—of or relating to the native, or original, peoples of Australia, who have lived there for at least 65,000 years

aquatic (uh-KWA-tik)—living in or growing in water

cryptid (KRIP-tid)—a creature whose existence has not been proven

fang (FANG)—a long, sharp tooth

folklore (FOHK-lor)—stories, traditions, and art forms of a specific people

prey (PRAY)—animals hunted by other animals as food

vampire (VAM-pire)—a creature that hunts in the night and drinks blood

READ MORE

Anderhagen, Anna. *Chasing the Chupacabra*. Minneapolis: Abdo Publishing, 2024.

Ha, Christine. *Chupacabra*. Mendota Heights, MN: Apex Press, 2022.

Long, Kim. *Catching Cryptids: The Scientific Search for Mysterious Creatures*. Philadelphia: Running Press Kids, 2025.

INTERNET SITES

American Museum of Natural History: Mythic Creatures Challenge
amnh.org/explore/ology/anthropology/mythic-creatures-challenge

American Museum of Natural History: Chupacabra
amnh.org/explore/ology/ology-cards/281-chupacabra

World Book: Beware the Bunyip
worldbook.com.au/bunyip/

INDEX

Aboriginal people, 8, 20
attacks, 18, 20, 24, 27
Australia, 6, 8

blood, 7, 10, 12, 22, 23

cave art, 10

fangs, 4, 16, 17, 27, 28
farm animals, 12, 22, 23
folklore, 8, 10

lakes, 8, 20

Mexico, 7, 10

prey, 18, 27
Puerto Rico, 7, 10, 12, 22

sightings, 6, 7, 8, 10, 12, 18, 20, 24

Taíno people, 10

United States, 7, 10

vampires, 10

ABOUT THE AUTHOR

Golriz Golkar is the author of more than 40 nonfiction books for children. Inspired by her work as an elementary school teacher, she loves to write the kinds of books that students are excited to read. Golriz holds a B.A. in American literature and culture from UCLA and an Ed.M. in language and literacy from the Harvard Graduate School of Education. She loves to travel and study languages. Golriz lives in France with her husband and young daughter, Ariane. She thinks children are the very best teachers and she loves learning from her daughter every day.